MW01253796

BORDER DEFENSE

Tony Hyland

✳

SEA-TO-SEA
Mankato Collingwood London

This edition first published in 2012 by
Sea-to-Sea Publications
Distributed by Black Rabbit Books
P.O. Box 3263, Mankato, Minnesota 56002

Printed in China

9 8 7 6 5 4 3 2

Published by arrangement with the Watts Publishing Group Ltd, London.

A CIP catalog record for this book is available from the Library of Congress.

ISBN: 978-1-59771-292-7

Series editor: Adrian Cole
Art director: Jonathan Hair
Design: Simon Borrough
Picture research: Luped

Acknowledgments:
Dita Alangkara/AP/Press Association Images: 14b. Marcel Antonisse/AFP/Getty Images: 10b. Petty Officer 3rd Class Annie R. Berlin/U.S. Coast Guard : 5b. L.Berns/vario images/Alamy: 27t. Alex Brandon/AP/Press Association Images: 13tr. Caro/Alamy: 27b. Paul Cooper/Rex Features: 23t. Charles Csavossy/U.S. Department of Homeland Security: 22. Mel Evans/AP/Press Association Images: 11b. Aaron Favila/AP/Press Association Images: 9. David R Frazier/Alamy: front cover. Sajjad Hussain/AFP/Getty Images: 28b. istockphoto: 29b Gerald L Nino/U.S. Department of Homeland Security: 4, 5cl, 6c, 8, 15b, 19t, 21t, 24, 25br. Photo courtesy of Northrop Grumman: 13c. Tim Ockenden/Press Association Images/PA Archive/Press Association Images: 18c. Denis Poroy/AP/Press Association Images: 7. Reuters: 1,14t,17b, 23b, 29t. Rex Features: 6b. Karim Sahib/ AFP/Getty Images: 26. Courtesy of the Serious Organised Crime Agency: 16. Sipa Press/Rex Features: 17c, 28t. James Tourtellotte/U.S. Department of Homeland Security: 10c, 11t, 12, 13tl, 15t, 18b, 19b, 20, 21b, 25l.

Every attempt has been made to clear copyright. Should there be any inadvertent omission please apply to the publisher for rectification.

February 2011
RD/6000006415/001

Contents

Words highlighted in the text can be found in the glossary.

Keeping Your Country Safe

Every country has borders. A border is the boundary around each country. Sometimes the border is marked by a high fence or other barrier, such as a river. Often the border is the sea coast around the country.

Part of the United States/Mexico border. The U.S. side is on the left.

Countries have laws to protect the people that live there. Laws help border officers to:

- Keep out illegal drugs
- Stop dangerous diseases from spreading
- Stop people who don't have permission to enter.

Many people work at the borders to keep their own country safe. Some inspect bags at airports. Others patrol the sea in ships or planes, looking for smugglers or anyone trying to enter the country illegally.

"Anti-terrorism is our primary mission but we are still focused on enforcement of immigration documents and illegal items." Arthur Gonzales, U.S. Customs and Border Protection, Acting Port Director, El Paso, Texas

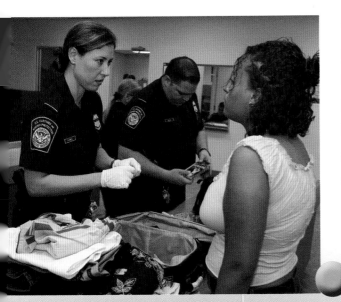

Customs officers inspect bags.

Coastguards on patrol in New York harbor.

The Protectors

There are many people working to protect our borders. They have different jobs that need special training and a range of skills.

Detection officers work at seaports, **land ports** and airports. They check everyone who enters the country. They look for people wanted by the authorities and people carrying illegal items, such as weapons. They also look for **illegal immigrants**.

Intelligence officers work behind the scenes. They gather information that assists in the detection of drugs and the arrest of smuggling gangs.

A detection officer conducts a search.

This X-ray shows people hiding in a truck. They are likely to be illegal immigrants.

Quarantine officers protect the country from dangerous diseases and pests. They check for people bringing in plants and seeds, as well as animals.

Coastguard officers patrol the sea. They watch for people trying to smuggle drugs or other goods by boat. They are also on the lookout for illegal immigrants.

ACTION STATS

The San Ysidro border crossing between Mexico and the U.S. (shown here) is the busiest in the world. An estimated 300,000 people use it each day.

Personal Gear

Border officers around the world wear different uniforms. They also use different equipment to do their jobs.

Detection officers usually wear lightweight clothing. In some countries they carry weapons. All officers have communications equipment to help them stay in contact with each other.

"A typical day involves selecting traffic, examining vehicles or passengers' baggage, and interviewing passengers to see if they have prohibited or restricted goods." Andy Dawe, UK detection officer

A detection officer checks a briefcase after it has been X-rayed.

AF FACTS

Smugglers use shoes with fake soles, hollowed-out religious books, and bags with secret compartments to hide illegal items.

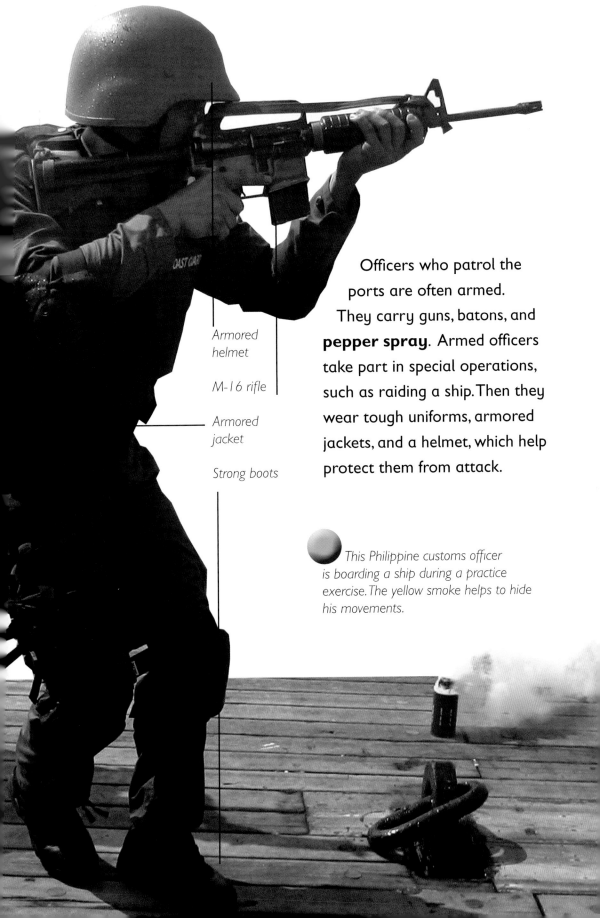

Armored
helmet

M-16 rifle

Armored
jacket

Strong boots

Officers who patrol the
ports are often armed.
They carry guns, batons, and
pepper spray. Armed officers
take part in special operations,
such as raiding a ship. Then they
wear tough uniforms, armored
jackets, and a helmet, which help
protect them from attack.

This Philippine customs officer
is boarding a ship during a practice
exercise. The yellow smoke helps to hide
his movements.

High-Tech Gear

Millions of people, vehicles, and packages pass legally across borders every year. Customs officers need extra equipment to check them carefully and quickly.

A U.S. Customs and Border Protection (USCBP) officer checks for illegal items as bags pass through a scanner.

A passenger walks through a metal detector.

At airports, officers use scanners so they can see things inside bags. They scan to find hidden guns and other illegal items. They check passengers for metal objects, such as knives, when they pass through a metal detector.

This mobile truck X-ray machine is being used to scan containers at a seaport.

Customs officers check cargo containers using large X-ray machines. Containers are filled with goods, but smugglers sometimes hide drugs and other illegal items inside a container. The X-ray machine makes it easy for officers to see anything unusual hidden inside.

AF FACTS

Hand-held detectors can be used to find dangerous items, such as explosives. This machine (left) measures tiny chemicals in the air, and can be used to find bombs.

On the Move

Officers patrol the air and sea in many different types of craft. Many countries cannot afford to buy all the equipment they need. This makes it harder to stop smugglers and terrorist activity.

ACTION STATS

The "Midnight Express" intercept vessel (below) is the most powerful of its kind. Top speed: 70 mph (III km/h • Range: 400 miles (643 km) • Length: 40 feet (12 m) • Power: 4 x 225 hp Mercury outboard motors

Large coastguard ships are called cutters. They often carry one or two helicopters and use **radar** to search the water and the sky.

Smaller, faster boats are used to intercept smugglers when they attempt to bring illegal items into a country.

Planes can travel quickly looking for any suspicious activity, such as a boat traveling at a very high speed. They alert ground units who can move in to intercept them.

Two U.S. Customs and Border Protection "Midnight Express" boats race to intercept a smuggler's speedboat.

Small jet planes are used to patrol coastal areas.

Coastguard helicopters have winches to lift people up quickly.

The Eagle Eye UAV is flown from cutters to assist in detection and search missions.

Helicopters cannot travel as far as planes, but they can fly and land in difficult places. Coastguard helicopters can be used to rescue people stranded at sea.

Unmanned Aerial Vehicles (UAVs) are planes that do not have a pilot. Officers control them from the ground. They can fly long distances, patrolling the border for many hours.

ACTION STATS

The Eagle Eye UAV can take off vertically. ● Top speed: 250 mph (400 km/h) ● Range: 125 miles (200 km) ● Length: 18 feet (5.5 m) ● Power: Allison 250-C20 GT turboshaft engine

Prohibited Imports

Laws ban people from bringing some items into a country. These items are called prohibited imports. **Knives, guns, and other weapons are usually prohibited imports because they are dangerous.**

These weapons were found hidden in a truck by Albanian border officers.

Many other items are not dangerous, but they are still prohibited. Illegal copies of console games, music, **counterfeit** money, and movies are all prohibited imports.

Smugglers hide prohibited items because they don't want border officers to find them. People can be fined or imprisoned if they are caught.

A customs officer in Jakarta, Indonesia, shows how surfboards were used to smuggle illegal drugs.

Officers work behind the scenes using high-tech gear to battle the smugglers. For example, **UV** detectors (left) can be used to find things that are not visible to normal vision, such as chemicals.

AF FACTS

Officers use drug analysis kits to find out what a suspicious substance really is. They place a tiny amount of it into the kit. If the substance is an illegal drug, the kit detects it immediately.

This drug test shows two pink tabs, which means the substance is not a drug.

MARIHUANA

Focus on:
Drug Smugglers

Stopping smuggling across the borders is a full-time job for border officers. Drug smugglers are right at the top of their target list.

There are many illegal drugs, such as heroin, cocaine, and ecstasy. Criminal gangs make money by selling the drugs. They smuggle different amounts, from a tiny fraction of an ounce to several tons.

Drugs gangs in parts of Africa use humans to transport small amounts of illegal drugs. They tape packets to their bodies underneath clothing. Others, called "drug mules," are promised money if they swallow sealed packages of drugs before traveling.

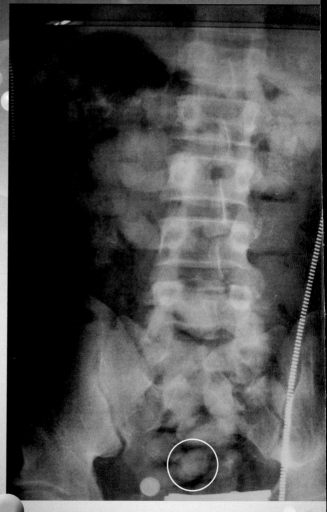

This X-ray shows the upper body of a drug mule. The lumpy areas (one is circled) are packets of drugs.

Arresting drugs smugglers and finding drugs takes a lot of work. Intelligence staff gather information about smuggling operations. Suspects can then be stopped as they try to smuggle items, and people in the gang can be arrested, too.

Customs officers arrest two suspects at a store in Mexico. Smuggling gangs usually have many members.

Detector Dogs

A dog's sense of smell is thought to be a thousand times better than a human's. Border defense officers use trained dogs to detect drugs and other prohibited items such as explosives, plants, food, and even cash.

A detector dog and handler on duty at an airport.

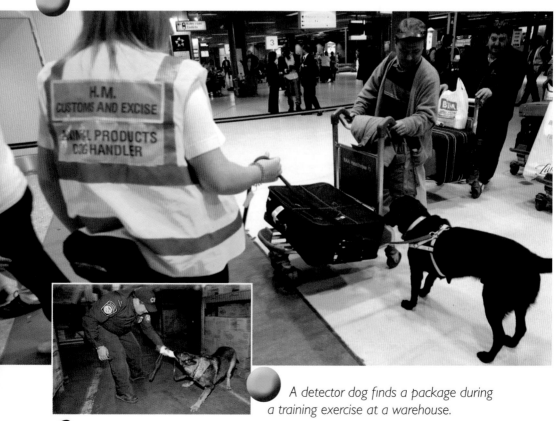

A detector dog finds a package during a training exercise at a warehouse.

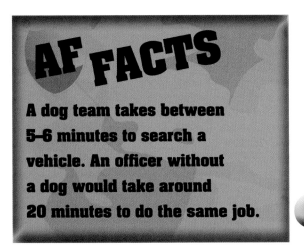

This car is being checked at a land port.

Dogs are trained on agility courses to get them ready to work at airports, ports, and other places. They climb over luggage and into cars, sniffing absolutely everything as they go along.

As soon as the dog detects a smell it has been trained to find, it stops and shows the handler where to look. The handlers reward the dog with a small treat.

This dog is taking part in an agility course as part of its training.

Airport Security

 A detection officer checks a passenger's passport.

Everyone who travels to another country by plane has to go through Customs. Officers look for prohibited items and also make sure passengers have paid duty, or tax, on legal items they bring in.

"The UK Border Agency is working hard to combat illegal immigration and Britain's border security has never been stronger."
David Holt, UK Border Agency

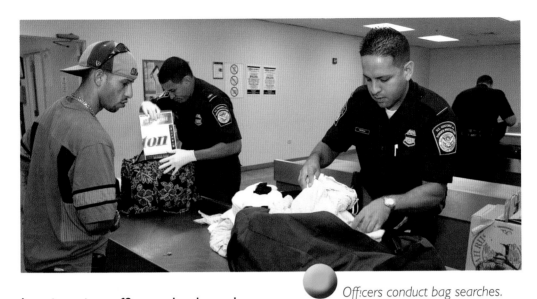

Officers conduct bag searches.

Immigration officers check each passenger's passport. This is a special document people need to enter and leave a country. They make sure that every passenger has the correct passport. Some people also need a visa. This is a document that allows people to work or stay for a set time.

Everyone has their bag checked by a scanner, but some are searched by hand. Officers may do this if a passenger has come from a particular country, or is known to the authorities.

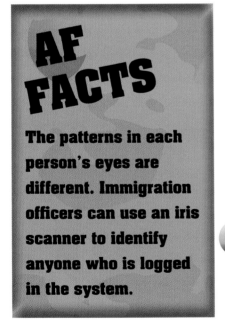

AF FACTS

The patterns in each person's eyes are different. Immigration officers can use an iris scanner to identify anyone who is logged in the system.

A passenger has his fingerprints scanned. This officer will also scan his iris to check his identity. Some countries keep records of iris scans.

Protecting the Seaports

Every day, ships bring thousands of tons of goods into the seaports of the world. Most of these goods are carried in metal boxes called containers.

This huge container ship is being unloaded at the Port of Los Angeles.

Customs officers patrol the ports. They check the goods that arrive. They search some containers for drugs or other smuggled items, but it is impossible to search them all.

A customs officer conducts a physical search of a container.

Customs officers also go on board ships and boats. They check that the sailors and passengers have the correct travel papers. They often climb around deep inside the ship, checking to see that there are no hidden items.

Turkish customs officers board a ship suspected of fuel smuggling.

Focus on:
U.S. Customs and Border Protection

The United States is a large, wealthy country and attracts many illegal migrants from countries in South and Central America. U.S. Customs and Border Protection (USCBP) work with authorities in Mexico to reduce the number of illegal people and items entering the U.S.

AF FACTS

There are around 7 million people living illegally in the U.S., often working in low-paid jobs and living in poor housing.

Suspected illegal immigrants are stopped by USCBP officers on the U.S. side of the U.S./Mexico border.

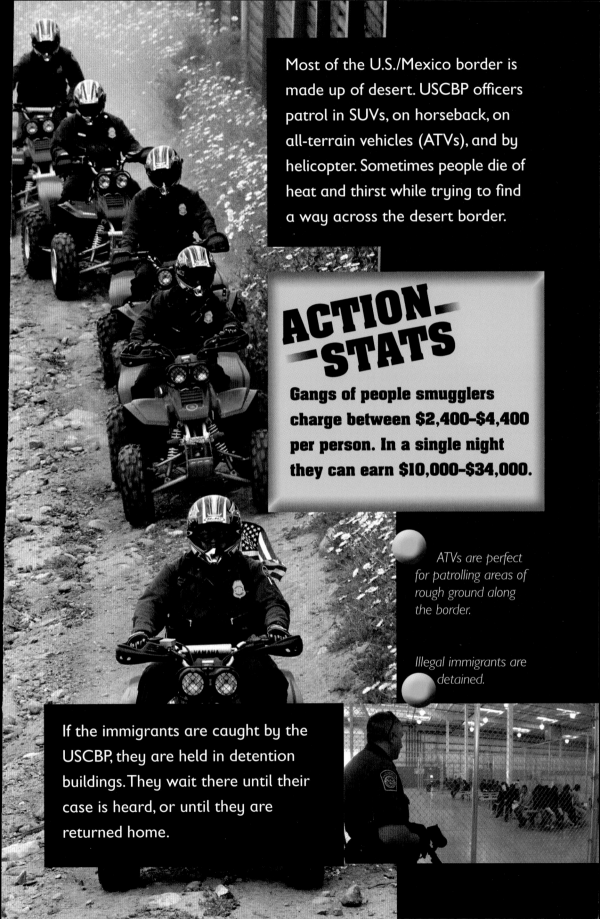

Most of the U.S./Mexico border is made up of desert. USCBP officers patrol in SUVs, on horseback, on all-terrain vehicles (ATVs), and by helicopter. Sometimes people die of heat and thirst while trying to find a way across the desert border.

ACTION STATS

Gangs of people smugglers charge between $2,400–$4,400 per person. In a single night they can earn $10,000–$34,000.

ATVs are perfect for patrolling areas of rough ground along the border.

Illegal immigrants are detained.

If the immigrants are caught by the USCBP, they are held in detention buildings. They wait there until their case is heard, or until they are returned home.

Illegal Workers

AF FACTS

In 2007, illegal workers in the United Arab Emirates (above) were given the chance to fly back home or to become legal migrants.

Every year, hundreds of thousands of people enter other countries illegally, hoping to find work. They usually come from poor countries, and want to earn more money. They get work in low-paid jobs, such as laborers on farms or on construction sites, or as cooks and cleaners in restaurants.

German police and customs officers (Zoll) raid a farm suspected of using illegal immigrant workers.

People smugglers often take advantage of these illegal workers. They pay the workers very low wages. They charge them large amounts of money for "protection." The illegal workers usually live in fear of being caught and returned to their homeland.

German officers search for evidence of illegal immigrants, passports, and emails.

Fighting Terrorism

A coastguard officer looks out across New York Harbor.

Terrorists try to cause as much death and destruction as they can. Often terrorist attacks are conducted by people from other countries. Border defense officers are on the lookout for anyone who may be trying to come into the country to commit terrorist acts.

Terrorist groups often try to get into India from Afghanistan and Pakistan. The border area is rough and mountainous country. It is very difficult to patrol. Indian Border Security Force officers patrol the area. They use planes and helicopters, as well as SUVs and ATVs.

Some borders, like this one between India and Pakistan, are heavily defended.

"We have caught two infiltrators trying to enter in the last two months." Major-General Tariq Yusuf, police chief of Iraq's Anbar province, which borders Syria

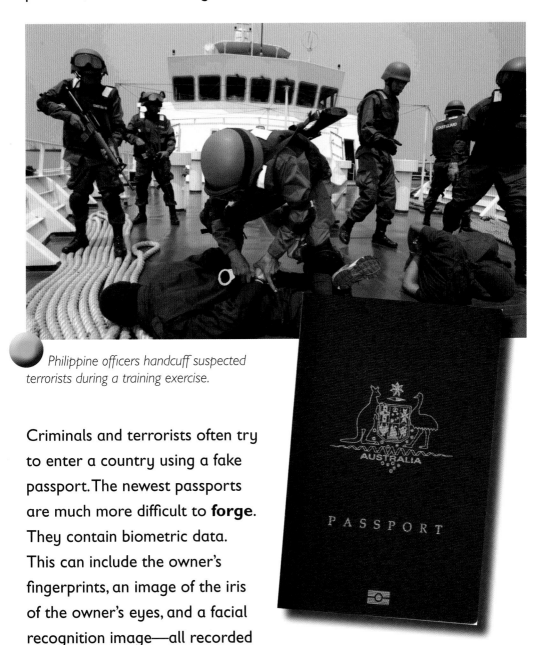

Philippine officers handcuff suspected terrorists during a training exercise.

Criminals and terrorists often try to enter a country using a fake passport. The newest passports are much more difficult to **forge**. They contain biometric data. This can include the owner's fingerprints, an image of the iris of the owner's eyes, and a facial recognition image—all recorded on a microchip. No two people have exactly the same biometric data.

This Australian passport has a symbol at the bottom of the cover to show it has a microchip in it.

Fast Facts

- There are about 11,000 U.S. Customs and Border Protection agents—89% work along the U.S./Mexico border. In contrast, there are 980 agents working along the U.S./Canada border.

- A man was arrested in Los Angeles in 2008 for smuggling three iguanas from Fiji. He hid them in his prosthetic leg, which he had hollowed out, before wearing it.

- In 2009, Spanish police seized $11 million in forged banknotes—the largest amount discovered to date.

- In 2009, the largest haul of heroin, valued at $12.76 million, was discovered at Heathrow Airport in the UK. It was hidden in holiday gifts sent from South Africa.

- Two pet dogs were used as drug mules when they had their stomachs stuffed with $200,000 worth of cocaine.

- In 2009, the UK Border Agency searched more than 200,000 freight vehicles to check for illegal and seized more than 22,000 people

Glossary and Web Sites

Counterfeit—an imitation of a product or document.

Forge—to make a false copy.

Illegal immigrant—a person who enters a country without permission.

Land port—a type of border station to control movement of people and goods from a country across land.

Pepper spray—a spray that makes the eyes stream and makes breathing difficult.

Prohibited import—a good that it is illegal to bring into a country, including illegal drugs, weapons, fake goods, or endangered animals.

Quarantine—a period of isolation for a person, animal, or plant to prevent the spread of disease.

Radar—a device that tracks planes and ships using radio waves.

UV (ultra violet)—a type of light ray invisible to the human eye.

www.cbp.gov/xp/cgov/border_security
This U.S. Customs and Border Protection web site features news videos of illegal goods seized, fact sheets, and a huge image gallery.

www.howstuffworks.com/airport-security.htm
Web page from howstuffworks showing you all the stages of airport security and how it works, plus an image gallery.

www.dhs.gov/files/counterterrorism.shtm
Find out more about counterterrorism operations on this web site of the U.S. Department of Homeland Security. It includes a link to the U.S. Coastguard web site.

Please note: every effort has been made by the Publishers to ensure that these web sites contain no inappropriate or offensive material. However, because of the nature of the Internet, it is impossible to guarantee that the contents of these sites will not be altered. We strongly advise that Internet access is supervised by a responsible adult.

Index